SOAR WITH WINGS LIKE EAGLES

VOLUME 2

DEDICATION

To **Ena Gomez**, my dear friend of 34 years, you are one in a million. She always caused me to look at myself and acknowledge the good and the bad. To her husband, **Ezra Gomez**, my late husband's childhood friend, for the unfailing support during my challenging times. They caused me to "SOAR - With Wings Like Eagles".

To my sister **Jennifer**, who made her home a haven of rest and tranquility for me for many months. To her husband, **Chris Sr.,** for being my chauffeur from Orlando to Suwanee, GA on a regular basis. To my nephew, **Chris Jr.**, for introducing me and providing a constant supply of the exotic teas he enjoys. Last, but not least, to my niece, **Monique**, who sacrificially gave up the luxury of her room to Aunty Marge for as long and as often as I wanted it.

To my special friends who supported and helped with the process of compiling this Publication; **Dr. Paul Zahl, Gina Joseph, Sydra Weston, Krystal Simmonds, Goldy Olivier, and Sarah Knight Pryor**. Thank you all for being so attentive and helpful.

A special "Thank you" and expressed appreciation to my Pastor, **Paula White-Cain**, who has been consistent in giving unwavering support in this season of my life. Contributing to my spiritual growth, maturity and walking in Destiny and purpose.

WITH WINGS LIKE EAGLES

Volume 2

A Collection of
Psalms, Poems & Spiritual Songs

MARGUERITE
REMY-ESANNASON

SOAR WITH WINGS LIKE EAGLES, VOLUME 2
Another Collection of Psalms, Poems & Spiritual Songs

Cover Design by Darrell A. Lobin

First Edition
ISBN: 978-0-615-19869-9

Printed in the United States of America.

10 9 8 7 6 5 4 3 2 1

Book Design by:
STALEON GROUP PUBLICATIONS
www.StaleonPublishing.com

TABLE OF CONTENTS

DEDICATION iii
INTRODUCTION ix
CHAPTER ONE 11
A CRY TO GOD FOR HELP 13
BLESSED BE THE LORD GOD, OUR SAVIOR 14
FAITH 16
GOD CALLING: A KIND OF DIALOGUE 17
GOD GOVERNS THE AFFAIRS OF MEN 19
GOD HAS MADE PROVISION 20
GOD IS ALWAYS ON TIME 21
HOPE 22
I INTEND TO DO YOUR WILL, O GOD 24
I STAND IN AWE OF YOU 26
IF YOU LIVE ACCORDING TO JESUS 27
JESUS IS MINE 28
JESUS, YOU ARE 29
JESUS, I KNOW YOU ARE ABLE 30
JESUS, YOU ARE MY ROCK 32
KNOW GOD 33
KNOWING GOD 34
MAGNIFY THE LORD WITH ME 35
MY FUTURE – MY CHOICE 36
MY TRIBUTE 38
NEVER AGAIN 39
THE CRY OF MY HEART 41
THE GREATNESS OF OUR GOD 42

THE LORD THY GOD, IS LORD OF ALL 43
THE LOVE WE GIVE 44
THE PROVISION OF GOD 45
THE WORD OF THE LORD 47
GOD IS LOVING, GOD IS KIND 48
YOU ARE ALL I NEED 50
TESTIMONIALS 51
SYDRA WESTON 53
COLVIN & JOY MCCALMAN 54
ANGELA LEWIS 55
ROSELLA SARACENI 56
ETHEL FOSTER COOLEY 57
JANE ROBESON 58
TERA DAHL 59
BERNADETTE GEORGE 60
EDDIE & LETTIE VASQUEZ 61
MONIQUE JACKSON 62
DR. PAUL ZAHL 63
BOBBY DELVECCHIO 65
BIOGRAPHY 67

INTRODUCTION

In the past two years of testing, isolation and uncertainty, after the release of my first book, *Soar With Wings Like Eagles - Volume One*, I watched the world move forward in uncertainty, and the spirit of fear grip so many. As I observed the uncertainty of life, the insecurity of man's decisions and the haphazard consequences of them, my heart was encouraged and strengthened with the truth and revelation of God's Word. I am referring to the scriptural theme of renewal described in Isaiah 40:31 (KJV), "They that wait upon the Lord; shall renew their strength; They shall mount up with wings as eagles; they shall run, and not be weary; and they shall walk and not faint."

This Word of the Lord will remain my testimony, the reservoir which the Spirit of the Lord poured into me for years and which will not return void no matter what is happening in the world around me.

Even in these precarious times, I believe that if we stand on the Word of God with unwavering resolve and faith, we will soar to new heights, new strength, living out the rest of our days in divine purpose and destiny.

In every moment of life, the only person who is with us, constantly promising never to leave us nor forsake us, is the Lord God Almighty Himself.

As you read and meditate on these revealed truths, may your heart Soar "With Wings Like Eagles, may you run and not be weary, and may you walk and not faint.

Marguerite Remy-Esannason

CHAPTER **ONE**

A CRY TO GOD FOR HELP

The flame in my heart is flickering,
The surge of power and life weakened.
I am caught up with too much around me.
Holy Spirit, draw me near, hold me close.
Holy Spirit, do not hold back.

Father, let your Word be the truth in my heart,
Let Your love fill me by the Holy Spirit.
Teach me to live for You and to die to myself.
Help me be willing and obedient to the things of God,
Not conformed to this world but transformed to Your way.

I confess my faults, my desires, my attitudes, my shortcomings.
I repent and turn around to please You every day that I live.
I follow You and do those things that are pleasing to You.
I am willing to die to myself, my desires, my wants.
Help me to stay on course, running the race with joy.

Keep my eyes from the unclean thing!
Keep my ears from corruption and my mind tuned into Your Word.
Keep my mouth that I may not speak perverse things.
I dedicate my life to You Who are the giver of life.
I give You my heart, my love, my attention and my praise.

Thank You, Father, for leading me on the straight way!
I choose Your way, I choose Your life, I choose Your Word.
Praying I dwell in Your presence in greater measure than it has ever been,
Praying that You hear and answer my prayer and my heart's desire,
Praying that You be pleased to answer me speedily.

August 16, 1988

BLESSED BE THE LORD GOD, OUR SAVIOR

Blessed be the Lord God, our Savior,
Who always causes us to triumph in Him.
Oh, give thanks to the Lord for He is good,
His mercy endures forever.

Today if you will hear His voice, harden not your hearts, answer Him.
Our eyes have not seen Him, but we know Him.
We know Him by His Name, by His Word, by His reputation.
We know Him when we do things in His honor and on His behalf.
We know Him when we do things because of Him.
Because He says to do it, we honor Him.

The sinners came to Him and were forgiven:
He will do the same for you.
The hungry came and were fed:
He will do the same for you.
The blind came and received their sight:
He will do the same for you.
Oh, give thanks to the Lord for He is good,
His mercy endures forever.

The demon-possessed came and He delivered them:
He will do the same for you.
The poor came and He made them rich:
He will do the same for you.
The lost came and He showed them the way:
He will do the same for you.
Oh, give thanks to the Lord for He is good,
His mercy endures forever.

The dead were raised to life by Him:
He will do the same for you.
The prostitutes came and He made them vessels of honor:
He will do the same for you.
The sick came and He healed them all:
He will do the same for you.
Oh, give thanks to the Lord for He is good,
His mercy endures forever.

The hypocrites came and He exposed them:
He will do the same for you.
The self-righteous came and He revealed them:
He will do the same for you.
The condemned came and He freed them:
He will do the same for you.
Oh, give thanks to the Lord for He is good,
His mercy endures forever.

Today, COME AS YOU ARE:
He will do the same for you.
Oh, give thanks to the Lord for He is good,
His mercy endures forever.
Blessed be the Lord God, Our Savior
Today and Forever.

April 30, 1988

FAITH

Thinking faith-thoughts and speaking faith-words
Will lead the heart out of defeat into victory.
Faith always has a good report.
Walk by faith and not by sight.

I am a faith-person.
I refuse to fear. I refuse to doubt.
I am a faith-child of a Faith God. My faith works!
I always have a good report. I refuse an evil report.

I am on God's side; He is on my side.
I belong to God, serve God, I am a child of God.
I believe God, I believe that it shall be
Even as it is written in His Holy Word.

God's Word cannot fail. I cannot fail.
I am standing on the promises of God.
Sincerely desire the benefits you ask of God,
Believing that what you ask is yours. God's Word works!

Whatsoever things you desire when you pray:
Believe that you receive them and you shall have them.
When other people's wills and desires are involved,
God's Hands of might and power will move the mountain.

Ask God in faith, nothing wavering. Stand your ground.
Call those things which are not as though they were.
Do not tolerate nor entertain for one single minute
A contrary thought to what you are believing for.

Count the things *done* that you have asked.
There is something about believing God
That will cause Him to pass over a million people to get to you.
Put His Word to the test. You will not be disappointed!
Exercise FAITH in spite of what you see or hear.

June 13, 1988

GOD CALLING: A KIND OF DIALOGUE

Lord, I am tired!

Yes, you are! You carry yourself around.
As much as I would have you lean on Me, you don't.
You believe you have to do it all yourself,
And even when you say you're tired.

Lean on Me, rest in Me.
Do not think 'what shall I wear?' or 'what shall I eat?'
I am the Good Shepherd. I will lead you and guide you.
I will go before you. Trust me and watch.
Didn't I say that if you trust Me, I shall come to your aid?

Did I not leave you a Helper? My Holy Spirit
One Who would work alongside you, and sustain you?
He will tell you whatever you're to say.
He will show you in the Spirit, things to come before they happen.
He will undertake what needs to be done. Step back.

.
When you are weak, He will be your strength.
When you are blind, He will give you sight.
Where you lack knowledge, He will give you revelation.
Where you lack understanding, He will give you wisdom.
Where you are in the dark, He will shed light.

There is nothing -- no, nothing -- that my Holy Spirit cannot do.
If you ask for His help, if you move in My purpose and plan,
The hour is now to do the works of God.
Work while the day is here, for the night comes,
When no one can work.

Grace has been multiplied to you, my dear child,
To proclaim liberty to the captives and to those who are bound.
Yes, I will do all that, and more!
Seek Me, stay in my Word, I will make things real to you.
I will make things come alive for you, and your mind will say YES.

Now tell Me this, are you still tired?
Now tell Me this, are you still tired?

April 1, 1086

GOD GOVERNS THE AFFAIRS OF MEN

God governs the affairs of men. Yes, He does!
He created the heavens and the earth
And all that is in them.
No one sees from His perspective.
No one governs the nations of the world as He does.

Yes, governments and rulers work within His purpose and His plan.
His position is a place of Authority and Reign.
He gives us liberty but in accordance with His ultimate design.
God has His agents governing and speaking His plans into existence,
His agents, His people declaring the Word of God.

The hearts of kings, rulers and presidents are in His hands.
He cannot be overruled or vetoed by anyone.
His ultimate plan and design will all be accomplished.
The Lord is high above all nations.

God is Judge over all.
Be Thou exalted, O God, above the Heavens.
Let Thy glory be over all the earth.
Your dominion is established forever. Who can change it?
Indeed, God governs the affairs of men.

September 28, 2020

GOD HAS MADE PROVISION

God has made provision for you.
You do not have to lean or depend on anyone else.
He will supply all your need
According to His riches in glory by Christ Jesus.

Seriously, know that God is your Provider.
You can experience His faithfulness to you,
His faithfulness in all the earth,
His faithfulness to all who will trust Him.

You do not have to agonize about your need. Trust!
Like the birds of the air and the creatures of the field:
They do not toil or labor, but God has made provision for them,
Caring for them better than King Solomon in all His glory.

God has made provision for your divine health.
Jesus took upon Himself your sicknesses and diseases.
By His stripes you are healed,
Redeemed from the curse of sickness and infirmity.

God is talking to you. Can you hear Him, can you see it?:
"Seek my face, look at Me.
I can do exceeding, abundantly, over all you will ask or think.
It is by My mighty power, which created the heavens and the earth."

As your Maker and Creator,
I have not left out a thing to give you abundant life.
I have made total provision for all you need.
I will complete in you what I have begun.
In fact, it is already done!
Completed, already in place, finished.

October 20, 2020

GOD IS ALWAYS ON TIME

God is always on time.
Never late, always on time.
Today if you hear His voice,
Harden not your heart as in the provocation,
As in the day of temptation in the wilderness.

God is always on time.
He sees the end from the beginning.
He governs the affairs of men.
He governs the affairs of earth.

Who has set the sun and moon on their schedule?
Who has set the seasons of the earth?
Who summons the snow, rain, hail and wind,
In their perfect time, in their perfect season?

Who has set the flowers to bloom, the trees to bear fruit,
The way of the eagles in the sky,
The way of the turtles as they deposit their eggs in the sand?
God and God alone, in His time.

To everything there is a season and a purpose under heaven,
A time to be born and a time to die,
A time to plant and a time to pluck up that which is planted,
A time to build up, a time to break down.

God has made everything beautiful in His time.
There is a time for every purpose and for every deed.
Oh God, have it Your way!
You are never late, ALWAYS ON TIME.

October 31, 2020

HOPE

We are NOT as those who have no HOPE.
HOPE in God and in His promises.
HOPE to live a daily, victorious and abundant life.
HOPE in the now and also in the future.
HOPE in the Hands of the Lord keeping us.
HOPE as our Father is the same yesterday, today and forever.

HOPE even though we walk through the fires of pain.
We shall not burn, neither will the flames consume us.
HOPE though we walk through deep waters, we will not drown.
HOPE in the mercy and compassion of Jesus.
HOPE in the God Who honors His Word.

HOPE in the future of eternal life.
HOPE as we grow and mature.
HOPE that God, Who never changes, yet is new every morning.
HOPE though the things we see and hear are constantly changing.
HOPE as we walk each day in the knowledge of an eternal future.
HOPE knowing that what God says will come to pass.

HOPE as thousands fall at our side and at our right hand,
HOPE it shall not come near us.
HOPE as God promises never to leave us, nor forsake us.
HOPE that the stripes of Christ have purchased our divine healing.
HOPE as God's thoughts towards us are countless,
HOPE as He has numbered the hairs on our heads.

HOPE because God's mercies are new every morning.
HOPE because He has sent us into the world for a purpose,
HOPE with a destiny to fulfil His will.
HOPE that the darkness around us will surely turn to light.
HOPE that God will open the seas for us to walk on dry land.
HOPE because the skies stay blue, and the sun rises every new day.

HOPE that God will give us the desires of our heart.
HOPE in Him with a life of Praise and Worship unto Him

HOPE in the love, joy and the peace He gives.
HOPE because His countenance reflects brightly upon our lives.
HOPE as God and Father will never lose His place of Supremacy.
We are NOT as those who have no HOPE.

January 21, 2021

I INTEND TO DO YOUR WILL, O GOD

A CRY TO GOD FROM A GRATEFUL HEART

I intend to do Your will, O God:
To walk in Your ways,
To follow Your paths,
To be Your witness,
A witness of Your love and mercy,
A witness to Your compassion.

I intend to do Your will, O God:
To reach out to the hurting,
To help the poor,
To be Your hands extended,
To be a vessel of honor for Your use,
To be a source of strength for the weak.

I intend to do Your will, O God:
To be a light in the darkness,
To comfort all who mourn,
To laugh with those who laugh,
To bring hope and be merciful,
To reach the lost at any cost.

I intend to do Your will, O God:
I will feed the hungry,
Clothe the naked,
Encourage the disheartened.
I will speak words of life and hope
To those who are hopeless.

I intend to do Your will, O God:
To give You glory and honor Your matchless Name,
To praise and worship You
For the great and mighty God You are

To the children of men, to all Your creation.
I intend to do Your will, O God.

September 17, 2020

I STAND IN AWE OF YOU

FROM A PLACE OF WORSHIP

Jesus, I stand in awe of You
Jesus, I stand in awe of You
I stand in awe of You
I stand in awe of You
I stand in awe of You

Breakthrough, I stand in awe of You
Breakthrough, I stand in awe of You
I stand in awe of You
I stand in awe of You
I stand in awe of You

You are a wonder; I stand in awe of You
You are a wonder; I stand in awe of You
I stand in awe of You
I stand in awe of You
I stand in awe of You

The Great I Am; I stand in awe of You
The Great I Am; I stand in awe of You
I stand in awe of You
I stand in awe of You
I stand in awe of You

Jesus, I stand in awe of You
Jesus, I stand in awe of You
I stand in awe of You
I stand in awe of You
I stand in awe of You

January 27, 2021

IF YOU LIVE ACCORDING TO JESUS (SONG)

If you live according to Jesus
He will give you His name (Repeat)
The Name above every other name.

If you live according to Jesus
The victory is yours (Repeat)
Victory over the enemy

If you live according to Jesus
You will never be alone (Repeat)
He will not leave you nor forsake You

If you live according to Jesus
You will not be afraid (Repeat)
His perfect love casts out all fear

October 5, 1987

JESUS IS MINE
(SONG)

Blessed assurance, Jesus is mine. (Repeat 3X)
Jesus is mine, He is mine.

Hallelujah, Jesus is mine. (Repeat 3X)
Jesus is mine, He is mine.

I'm so glad, Jesus is mine. (Repeat 3X)
Jesus is mine, He is mine.

Praise His Name, Jesus is mine. (Repeat 3X)
Jesus is mine, He is mine.

I bless You, Lord, Jesus is mine. (Repeat 3X)
Jesus is mine, He is mine.

Holy, holy, holy, Jesus is mine. (Repeat 3X)
Jesus is mine, He is mine.

Receive my praise, For Jesus, You're mine. (Repeat 3X)
Jesus, You're mine, Jesus, You're mine.

June 17, 1985

JESUS, YOU ARE

Jesus, You are my Savior, saving me daily, consistently.
Jesus, You are my Redeemer, buying back my life from destruction.
Jesus, You are my Deliverer, rescuing me from day-to-day.
Jesus, You are my Comforter, consoling me when I am sad.

Jesus, You are my Shelter, in the time of storm.
Jesus, You are my Friend, who sticks closer than a brother.
Jesus, You are my Stabilizer, in times of uncertainty.
Jesus, You are my Healer, when I am sick, and tired.

Jesus, You are my Rock, keeping me secure, unmovable.
Jesus, You are my Hope in times of anxiety.
Jesus, You are my Light when darkness is all around.
Jesus, You are my Peace in the midst of uproar.

Jesus, You are my Compass, when I have lost my direction.
Jesus, You are my Inspiration in the midst of doubt and fear.
Jesus, You are my Sustainer, when I am lacking and needy.
Jesus, You are my Victory, overcoming every obstacle.
Jesus, You are ALL I need, today and tomorrow and forever.

May 28, 1985

JESUS, I KNOW YOU ARE ABLE (SONG)

CHORUS:
Jesus, I ill cling to You, come what may,
I know You are able, I know You are true
I know You are able, I know You are true

Jesus, I know You are able to bring me through this wilderness.
I know You are able to bring me through this desert.
Jesus, You are the Way, the Truth and the Life.
You are the living water in a dry and thirsty land.
I know You are able.

Jesus, I know You are able to turn the water into wine,
The anointing that you freely give to all who will receive.
Jesus, I know You are able to walk with me through the darkness.
You are the Light of the world, lighting my path.
I know You are able.

Jesus, I know You are able to calm the wind and the waves.
You walked on water and caused creation to submit.
Jesus, You are the bright and Morning Star.
You are the hope of the nations and the promised Messiah. I know You are able.

Jesus, I know You are able to make me stand secure.
You are the Solid Rock on which I stand.
I walk through the valley of the shadow of death with no fear.
You are the Savior of the world, conquering death and hell.
I know You are able.

Jesus, I know You are able to give me new life.
You rose from the dead and live forever more,
Seated at the right hand of God the Almighty, our Majesty on High.
You have not lost Your position, King of Kings and Lord of Lords. I

know You are able.

Jesus, I know You are able for all creation declares Your majesty.
With our eyes we see Your glory.
You hold all things with the Word of Your power,
With majesty and splendor You come for Your Bride, the Church
I know You are able! I know You will!

October 10, 2020

JESUS, YOU ARE MY ROCK

I can do all things, through Christ Who strengthens me
You are my rock; Jesus You are my Rock
You are my rock; Jesus You are my Rock

I can run through a troop and leap over walls
You are my rock; Jesus You are my Rock
You are my rock; Jesus You are my Rock

I am more than a conqueror, by the power of Your name
You are my rock; Jesus You are my Rock
You are my rock; Jesus You are my Rock

I am seated in heavenly places in You
You are my rock; Jesus You are my Rock
You are my rock; Jesus You are my Rock

I am strong in the Lord and in the power of Your might
You are my rock; Jesus You are my Rock
You are my rock; Jesus You are my Rock

I have authority in Your Name and by Your Blood
You are my rock; Jesus You are my Rock
You are my rock; Jesus You are my Rock

September 21, 2021

KNOW GOD

KNOW GOD for Who He is,
The great Creator, Almighty God,
The One, Who alone stands in glory and majesty,
Who governs all things by the Word of His power.

KNOW GOD for yourself: Seek Him, run after Him, find Him.
Know Him in His might, in His power and His truth.
Let the reality of Who He is consume your heart and life.
KNOW your Creator, the Ruler of the entire universe.

KNOW GOD, He was and is and will forever be.
He is the sustainer of the whole universe.
Call upon Him, spend time with Him.
He will reveal Himself to you.

KNOW GOD, set aside time with Him,
Set aside time to listen to Him.
Give Him glory, honor and the praise He deserves.
KNOW GOD and encourage others to know Him also.

KNOW GOD, your life depends on Him,
Your quality of life depends on knowing Him.
Build a relationship with Him and be quiet before Him.
Know His Voice, know His Mind and feel His Heart.

KNOW GOD, there is a place of no return
When you engulf yourself and engage in a relationship with Him.
The experience is infinite, rewarding, peaceful and complete.

KNOW GOD - KNOW **"THE I-AM, THAT I AM".**

October 7, 2021

KNOWING GOD

Knowing who God is,
Knowing who God says He is,
Knowing Him and His fullness,
Knowing Him in truth,
Knowing Him is revolutionary!

Knowing Him in the good times,
Knowing Him in the not-so-good times,
Knowing Him when I rise,
Knowing Him when I lie down at night,
Knowing Him when I am alone, or in a crowd.

Knowing God is to be like Him.
Knowing God is to love like Him.
Knowing God is to talk and act like Him.
Knowing God is to be a witness for Him.
Knowing God is to spend quality time with Him.

Increasing in the knowledge of God is an everyday task.
This is how relationship are built
Not by works doing, but relationship is more important to Him,
Being like Him, loving, kind, merciful,
Gentle, long-suffering with self-control,
Exercising goodness and holiness.
You will come to be like Him.
Be like God today!

August 31, 2020

MAGNIFY THE LORD WITH ME

My soul doth magnify the Lord,
My spirit rejoices in God my Savior,
For He that is mighty has done great things, and Holy is His name.
His mercy is from everlasting to everlasting to them that fear Him.

The Lord is my portion, He it is Who leads me.
He it is Who gives me breath.
He sets me up on my high places
All glory and honor is His.

Who is like Him?
Who can span the oceans with their hands?
Who can make the heavens their home?
Who can breathe life into us so we live?
Who can control the universe by the Word of His power?

It is He who rides above the heavens by His Name: Jehovah.
He causes me to have victory over my enemies,
Over those who set traps for my soul and snares for my feet,
Those who would cause me to stumble.

I am free to worship and adore Him!
Through His great love, His unfailing, never-ending love,
Drawing me into His Presence, day by day,
Revealing His Greatness and Glory of His Majesty.

His Holy Spirit draws us near to Him,
To feel His power, to know His love, to experience His presence.
The Great I Am, the I AM, anything you want Him to be.
Come magnify the Lord with me. Let us exalt His name together!

April 16, 1988

MY FUTURE – MY CHOICE

My future is my choice
My salvation is in no one's hands but mine.

God has demonstrated His love for me
For while I was yet in sin Christ died for me.
For God so loved the world that He gave His only begotten Son
That who believes in Him will not perish but have everlasting life.
Nothing can separate me from the love of God which is in Christ Jesus, our Lord.
I choose to receive His love and forgiveness.

God has made provision and given me divine health
For Jesus was wounded for my transgressions
He was bruised for my iniquities and with His stripes I am healed.
Jesus took upon Himself my sickness and my infirmities.
Jesus healed the sick and all those who were oppressed by the devil
I choose to receive His healing.

God has delivered me from every evil plan of the enemy.
For the Lord shall deliver me from every evil work.
He will preserve me unto His heavenly Kingdom.
He has delivered me from the power of darkness
And translated me into the Kingdom of His dear Son.
I choose to receive His deliverance.

God has given me prosperity, as He supplies all my needs
According to His riches in Glory by Christ Jesus.
He became poor that I might rich and help others.
I will obey the Lord and serve Him,
I will spend my days in prosperity and my years in pleasures.
I choose to receive His prosperity.

God protects me from all evil.
No evil shall befall me, neither shall any plague come to my dwelling
God has given His angles charge over me, to keep me in all my ways.

In all these things I am more than a conqueror through Him
He makes a way in the wilderness and rivers to flow in the desert.
I choose to receive His protection.

God has given me His power
Power to live a victorious life
Power in His Name to overcome obstacles and challenges
Power to deliver and set free those who are bound
Power over all the power and influence of the enemy.
I choose to receive His power.

God has created me to Worship Him
To worship Him in the beauty of holiness
To worship Him in spirit and truth
To worship and honor Him as the One True, Living God
To worship Him, the Creator of the world and all therein
I choose to worship God.

God deserves my praise and adoration
Praise the Lord O my soul, praise His Holy Name
I bless the Lord at all times, His praise will always be in my mouth.
Praise the Lord oh my soul and forget not all His benefits.
Yes, I will praise the Lord with all my whole heart and soul.
I choose to praise and adore God.

December 4, 2021

MY TRIBUTE

TO HIM WHO REIGNS FOREVER AND EVER

Though I was distressed, You have lifted me up.
Though I was falling, You have grabbed hold of me.
Though I was weak, Your strength has become my strength.
In Thee do I trust, O Lord,
Your faithfulness exceeds my understanding,
Your light and Your presence dispel my darkest hour.
All glory and praise to You,
For truly You are the Holy One of Israel.
The One to Whom creation bows,
The One to Whom trees clap their hands,
The rivers sing, the birds praise.
All glory and honor is Yours,
Almighty Father, Who was and is and is to come, Forever and ever.

March 19, 1987

NEVER AGAIN

Never again will I confess I can't,
For *"I can do all things through Christ, Who strengthens me"*.

Never again will I confess lack,
For *"My God shall supply all my needs according to His riches in Christ Jesus"*.

Never again will I confess fear,
For *"God has not given me the spirit of fear, but of power and love and of a sound mind"*.

Never again will I confess doubt and lack of faith,
For "God has given to every man the measure of faith".

Never again will I confess weakness,
For *"The Lord is the strength of my life"*.

Never again will I confess the power of Satan over my life,
For *"Greater is He that is within me than he that is in the world"*.

Never again will I confess defeat,
For *"God causes me always to triumph in Christ Jesus"*.

Never again will I confess confusion and ignorance,
For *"Jesus Christ is made unto me wisdom from God"*.

Never again will I confess sickness,
For *"With His stripes I am healed"*.

Never again will confess worries and anxiety,
For *"I am casting all my cares on Him, for He cares for me"*.

Never again will I confess bondage and inadequacies,
For *"Where the Spirit of the Lord is, there is liberty"*.

Never again will I confess condemnation, guilt and self-judgment,

For *"There is therefore now no condemnation to those who are in Christ Jesus"*.

I am Free! Free! Free!

June 30, 1982

THE CRY OF MY HEART

Lord, I am not exactly sure what I need.
But this I know, I need You, I want You.
I need a fresh and clear revelation of Who You are.
On my honor I promise to do my best, as long as I live,
To seek the knowledge of God,
The promise of God, the security of God, the life of God,
The peace of God, the direction of God.
To make Your Word, my word, the life of God, my life,
To know Your direction for my life,
To feel Your Heart and know Your Mind.
Lord, I love You. I need Your help; I need Your peace.
I need discernment, direction.
I need to know how to pray, how to seek Your face.
I need to exercise Your Love, Your Patience.
Fill the void in my life and have Your character be a part of me.
Pour out Your Spirit upon me to fulfill Your purposes in my life.

March 17, 1988

THE GREATNESS OF OUR GOD

God in His greatness and power –
He took dirt and dust, and made man.
He took words and created a galaxy.
He shaped the earth round so that it spins on its axis.

He placed the sky and the clouds in the heavens.
He created the sun, moon and stars.
He set the oceans and seas in place
And gave them their boundaries.

He is light and life.
He moves mountains with words.
He died yet He lives.
He gave man life with the breath of His nostrils.

He sent fire down from heaven.
He closed the lion's mouth.
He parted the Red Sea.
He resurrected the dead.

He made the lame walk again.
He opened blinded eyes.
He took dry bones and made them live again.
He gave adults new birth.

He commands angels and gives them assignments.
He forgets confessed sins.
He cannot lie, His words always come to pass.
His thoughts always come true.

Oh, the greatness of God!
Who can overcome HIM? NO ONE.

November 4, 2020

THE LORD THY GOD, IS LORD OF ALL (SONG)

Hear oh earth, hear oh earth,
The Lord thy God. He is One Lord of All
He is one, one God, one Lord and Master of all.
The Lord Thy God is Lord of all

The Shepherd of the flock.
The Lord thy God, He is one God.
Worship and adore Him, reverence Him all the earth.
The Lord Thy God is Lord of all

Give Him glory, give Him praise
To the true and living God.
Bow down to the King of Kings, the Lord of Lords
The Lord Thy God is Lord of all

Praises to the King of Kings.
Praises to the Lord of Lords.
Worship and bow down all the earth.
The Lord Thy God is Lord of all

To Him be all of the glory.
To Him be all of the praise.
To Him be all of the praise, Hallelujah!
To Him be all of the glory.
To Him be all of the praise.
To Him all of the praise, Hallelujah!

December 20, 2020

THE LOVE WE GIVE

DEDICATED TO PASTOR PAULA WHITE-CAIN

The love we give - Will reflect on Who God is.
The love we give - Will describe the One Who is greater than we are.

The love we give – Will give hope to others.
The love we give - Will encourage others to cling to life in the face of loss.

The love we give - Will give hope to those in despair.
The love we give - Will strengthen the faint of heart.

The love we give - Will shine bright and dispel the darkness.
The love we give - Will heal the sick.

The love we give - Will spark others to give and share.
The love we give - Will make miracles happen!

The love we give - Will always revisit our lives.
The love we give - Will shine through our lives and bless us.

The love we give - Will bring redemption to those around us.
The love we give - Will change the world.

The love we give - Will cover a multitude of sins.
The love we give - Will kindle in people the desire to embrace their life.

November 12, 2020

THE PROVISION OF GOD

God took His children out of bondage,
Out of slavery, working seven days a week,
No time laid aside for Him or for their families.
He brought them to a land flowing with milk and honey,
Gave each person an inheritance: No toil, No sweat, Servants to do the work and a full day's rest, Unlike anything they'd ever known.

An inheritance He gave them from their enemies,
Who were also His enemies.
Today I believe God can do the same:
Take our enemies and make them our servants.
Take the inheritance from them and give it to us,
The wealth of the wicked given to the just.
We won't be slaves to them and their world system.

With this inheritance we can be like the Jews:
The ransomed People of God going to the Temple
Three times a day, to pray, discuss His Word and learn His ways.
No wonder the Romans placed such heavy taxes on them.
They had so much and could afford to pay.
Jesus sent Peter to get their tax money from a fish:
No toil, No sweat.

Can God do the same for us today?
Can He take us out of bondage and give us an inheritance?
Can He give us victory over our enemies?
Can He take us out of slavery?
Can He make our enemies our slaves?
Can He give us that liberty?
Yes, He can! He has made provision.

Can God take the wealth of the wicked and give it to the just,
The righteous ones, in His Name? Can He? Will He?
We know from His Word that He has no favorites.
What He has done for others, He can do the same for you.

Can we look to God and claim that promise?
Can we dare? Yes, we can!!!
Walk in the liberty whereby Christ has made us free!!!!

March 24, 1988

THE WORD OF THE LORD

I am calling upon you to heed My Word.
There is direction in My Word,
There is life in My Word,
My Word is truth.

My Word will direct you when your eyes cannot see
My Word will speak to you when your ears cannot hear.
Feed on My Word, yield to My Word.
My Word, it will give you direction.

My Word will direct you on the path I have laid out for you,
The path I have laid out for your life.
Direction will come,
Instruction will come.

Follow My Word and find your destiny.
Follow and find your purpose.
Follow and find My will for your life.
My Word will give victory in every circumstance.

My Word will come alive to those around you,
Those who look to you.
And to those to whom I will send you,
My Word will bring life and bear fruit in your life,
Sayeth your God and King!

November 25, 2020

GOD IS LOVING, GOD IS KIND

God is loving, God is kind,
The One who never leaves a single one behind.
Get to know Him:
Your life will never be the same,
Never be the same.
See Him demonstrate His love beyond imagination

God is loving, God is kind.
You will get to understand Him. You will build a solid life on Who He is, And on the greatness of His might.
You will draw closer and closer
To the point where you cannot live without Him.

God is loving, God is kind.
He brightens every shadow and lifts every burden.
He gives you wings to fly like an eagle.
Your heart and mind will have rest and peace in Him,
In Him who is near and close to your heart.
You will see the world through His eyes.

God is loving, God is kind.
He will erase your past and give you new life.
He will reveal His divine plan to you.
Your impossibilities will vanish.
He will direct your destiny,
Opening new doors of opportunity before you.

God is loving, God is kind.
Be His vessel, be His representative.
Seek Him, hear Him, obey Him.
Victory will be yours,
Life will take on new meaning
New heights, new goals achieved.

God is loving, God is kind.
He will meet your need and satisfy your soul.
He will always be near, closer than a brother,
Knowing what you do not know and working for your good.
His thoughts are always about you:
His eyes, His gaze constantly on you.

God is loving, God is kind.
Live life in Him.

October 2, 2020

YOU ARE ALL I NEED

I found my joy in You,
I found my hope in You,
I found my security in You,
I found my peace in You.

Your love is so encompassing, so compelling,
Leaving me no doubt or question You are near,
You are forever with me, never to leave me.
That you care! Really care!

Your encompassing love and security
Takes away every thought or feeling of loneliness and emptiness.
They vanish when You grace me with Your presence,
So fulfilling and satisfying as Your comfort surrounds me.

Your security is undeniable and humbling
You in all Your splendor and majesty,
You Who hold the whole world in the palm of Your hand
Would grace me with Your Presence - Your Glory!

Your limitless love, grace, favor and abounding mercies
Reconcile me to You daily, they are new each day,
Daily in Your rest,
Daily in Your care,
Daily in Your love.

August 23, 2021

TESTIMONIALS

SYDRA WESTON

This book is true intimacy with God. The sweetness of God's presence is poured out on every page. So pure and eloquently written, Elder Marguerite Remy-Esannason's poems are nothing but the expression of God's Love. If you are looking for closeness in your quiet times with God, look no further; Soar with Wings Like Eagles will surely elevate you to the highest intimacy with our Heavenly Father.

Sydra L. Weston

Author, *Dating While Waiting; Staying Pure to Your Purity Vow*

COLVIN & JOY MCCALMAN

Volume one was well written, easy to read and inspirational. Sharing what God gave you was not for yourself but for others. The entire book was very GOOOOD. Section five, "Life with God" was my favorite and meaningful to me, especially [the line], "I want to brag on you." Thanks for being obedient. You have always been an inspiration to us.

Colvin & Joy McCalman

Angela Lewis

SOAR With Wings Like Eagles, Volume 1 helped me to grow more in wisdom, develop strong Christian character and become stronger in my faith. The Volume 1 book gives me peace and joy in my heart.

I would encourage you to purchase Volume 2. I believe it will transform your life. Every person who reads this book will be blessed.

Thank you, Elder Marguerite. I am honored and grateful to be part of your book. Thank you, Jesus.

Angela Lewis

Rosella Saraceni

SOAR With Wings Like Eagles, is a journey to deeper intimacy with God. Marguerite captures the very essence of our Father in the declarations and promises from the Living Word that is our anchor of Love. The seasons of life change BUT our God's love for us never changes. This book is a profound reminder that God works in us and through us to be a blessing of encouragement to each other. Divine timing caused this book to cross my path at a time where I so needed this reminder and as Marguerite so profoundly declares: "Brag on Jesus" as He is our strength in all seasons!

Rosella Saraceni

ETHEL FOSTER COOLEY

In Elder Marg's first volume of *SOAR With Wings Like Eagles*, I feel that God has given her anointed hands and a mind to put her words to print. As I read each Psalm, each poem and each Spiritual song, I knew it had to be a gift from God to enable the Elder to touch the hearts of many through this publication.

It has been uplifting, inspiring and encouraging, giving me hope for brighter days ahead no matter the situation. It is a phenomenal and powerful volume that can be a witnessing tool.

Ethel Foster Cooley

JANE ROBESON

After I received your request, I decided to read your book again. I love how you can totally immerse yourself in the presence of God, while reading this book. It's like being on a retreat to freshen your soul and reminds us why we are to pursue our first love. It absolutely brings the joy of the Lord, (which is our strength) and as we find that strength, we SOAR!!

Jane Robeson

Tera Dahl

"Reading Marguerite's book, *SOAR With Wings Like Eagles*, was inspirational and touched my heart. It helped me to remember that no matter what we go through in life, God has given us the strength to fulfill His calling and purpose in our life. We can trust in God's presence and promises to guide us and lead us every day of our lives. I highly recommend everyone to read her inspiring words!"

Tera Dahl

BERNADETTE GEORGE

Soar With Wings Like Eagles: A Collection of Psalms, Poems & Spiritual Songs is a book with a different twist on learning about who God really is. With inspirational poems from the heart and a touch of a personal journey with God, it's a must read because it not only touches you spiritually but emotionally as well. The author has a creative mind and draws you into the biblical meaning of the word of God.

Bernadette George

EDDIE & LETTIE VASQUEZ

Heartwarming and Beautifully Written.

My wife and I have wanted to get to know GOD more intimately and this book definitely opened up our hearts to Him. Anyone that reads this book will experience their own unique encounter with GOD. Each chapter stands alone and can be read independently. You can go directly to any chapter and feel in your heart GOD is speaking to you.

This book is beautifully written. We highly recommend it. GOD BLESS YOU Elder Marguerite and we look forward to your next book.

Eddie & Lettie Vasquez

MONIQUE JACKSON

Uplifting, powerful, and thought-provoking are the first three words that came to mind as I read *SOAR With Wings Like Eagles*. There is a calmness that comes when you read the first three poems in this inspirational book especially. One of the common denominators that serves as the forefront of this book is faith. The elegant use of scripture mixed with words of encouragement left me with a yearning to strengthen my faith but also encouraged me to look to scripture and never lose faith in God in my times of need.

Monique Jackson

DR. PAUL ZAHL

It's a salubrious moment to anticipate this new volume of Elder Marguerite Esannason's poetry. Her work is faith-building and joy-creating.

Why do I say that? Well, partly because of the author herself, who walks and talks with God. She is a very real person who actually relates in the matters, big and small, of her everyday life with a personal, solace-bearing God.

Thus, Elder's poems are coming from a real place! They are not conceptions or manufactured chariots of rhetoric. No, they are cries, pleas and affirmations from the heart of a woman who is... all heart.

Sometimes I like to compare Elder Marguerite's heart-riven poems to the short, sweet and simple poems of our 18th-Century forebears like William Cowper and John Newton. Those men also wrote from the heart, for they just said what they had to say, without artifice or looking for human praise. Moreover, they wrote for actual congregations in the same way Elder M. is in ministry with actual people, suffering and aspiring souls, every day of her life.

In short, the Elder's work is utterly lacking in pretense, suffused with the sincerity of committed pastoral care, and inspiringly saturated with the written Word of God and its continuing power to aid us... to soar.

Dr. Paul Zahl

BOBBY DELVECCHIO

Soar - With Wings Like Eagles Volume 2. Put this book on your calendar to buy and learn about the journey of this amazing woman who has done more for humanity than most Nobel laureates!

As long as I've known Elder Marguerite, I've been a big fan. She has a heart of gold and wisdom beyond her years- truly a saint and a servant of the Lord. Her first book, *Soar With Wings Like Eagles*, was so profound that I read it daily to inspire me to a higher spiritual life.

Bobby Delvecchio

BIOGRAPHY

Marguerite Remy-Esannason is a Christian leader of over 40 years' service and experience. She was one of the very First Elders ordained for New Destiny Christian Center, now City of Destiny, in Apopka, Florida and has been a member and part of the Pastoral Team for over 26 years.

Prior to New Destiny, Elder Marguerite served Faith Christian Fellowship Church in St. Thomas, US Virgin Islands; and prior to that, she worked and also served at Queensway Cathedral in Toronto, Canada, where she lived for 19 years.

Elder Marguerite was born on the island of St. Lucia, West Indies, where she was the eldest of 12 children from beloved and devout Roman Catholic parents. She attended Catholic schools before immigrating to Canada in 1968. It was in Toronto that she was saved, receiving Jesus as her personal Savior, and where she received her call to the ministry.

Behind her decades of public ministry and pastoral care, Elder Marguerite's sustaining faith has expressed itself in quiet private writings, mostly hymns and psalms and spiritual songs. These consoling and strengthening poems have held a part of her devoted heart -- and her most personal experience of God -- that the world has not seen. Yet in the recent past, partly as the result of personal losses, she has been called to publish them, as a help to others who are also living life in the light of God's Grace.

This *SOAR – With Wings Like Eagles, Volume 2* is a sharing from the heart of Elder Marguerite. Walk with her now, in the everyday life of a real Christian woman, and let her words speak to you in your own walk, in its dry places and in its joys.

Staleon Group

Made in the USA
Coppell, TX
06 July 2022